BIG MACHINES FOR BIG JOBS
FIRE TRUCKS
ON THE JOB
FOGGY BOTTOM
23
RYAN JAMES
NORWOOD HOUSE PRESS

Cataloging-in-Publication Data

Names: James, Ryan.
Title: Fire trucks on the job / Ryan James.
Description: Buffalo, NY : Norwood House Press, 2026. | Series: Big machines for big jobs | Includes glossary and index.
Identifiers: ISBN 9781978573840 (pbk.) | ISBN 9781978573857 (library bound) | ISBN 9781978573864 (ebook)
Subjects: LCSH: Fire engines--Juvenile literature.
Classification: LCC TH9372.J359 2026 | DDC 629.225--dc23

Published in 2026 by
Norwood House Press
2544 Clinton Street
Buffalo, NY 14224

Copyright © 2026 Norwood House Press
Designer: Rhea Magaro
Editor: Kim Thompson

Photo credits: Cover, p. 1 Nicole Glass Photography/Shutterstock.com; p. 3 Antonio Galvez Lopez/Shutterstock.com; p. 5 Karolis Kavolelis/Shutterstock.com; p. 6 Monkey Business Images/Shutterstock.com; p. 7 Kazela/Shutterstock.com; p. 9 Ron Zmiri/Shutterstock.com; p. 10, 11 Gorodenkoff/Shutterstock.com; p. 12 Mike Brake/Shutterstock.com; p. 13 Brian Logan Photography/Shutterstock.com; p. 15 ChiccoDodiFC/Shutterstock.com; p. 16 Maria Sbytova/Shutterstock.com; p. 18 Just dance/Shutterstock.com; p. 19 New Africa/Shutterstock.com; p. 21 Jerry Sharp/Shutterstock.com;

Printed in the United States of America

Some of the images in this book illustrate individuals who are models. The depictions do not imply actual situations or events.

CPSIA compliance information: Batch #CSNHP26: For further information contact Norwood House Press at 1-800-237-9932.

Find us on 

TABLE OF CONTENTS

PARTS OF A FIRE TRUCK

Fire trucks are big machines. They have **flashing** lights. They have **sirens**.

PIZZA
F.D. N.Y.
26
SP14004
BATMAN

The front of the truck has a cab. The driver and other firefighters sit there.

There is a long ladder that **telescopes**.

It can reach the tops of tall buildings.

The truck also carries shorter ladders.

Tools are kept on the sides of the truck. There are **axes**, hoses, and **fire extinguishers**.

WHAT DOES A FIRE TRUCK DO?

Fire trucks help in **emergencies**. They come quickly. They help put out fires. They help **rescue** people.

When a fire truck is going to an emergency, its lights and sirens are on. Drivers on the road must let the fire truck pass.

WHAT DOES A FIRE TRUCK DO?

Fire trucks help in **emergencies**. They come quickly. They help put out fires. They help **rescue** people.

Fire trucks have big water tanks inside. Shorter hoses and jets **connect** to this tank. They help firefighters put out small fires quickly.

Longer hoses connect to a fire **hydrant**. This provides lots of water for putting out large fires.

A ladder basket helps firefighters get to high places. They can open windows on burning buildings. They can reach people who are trapped.

FIRE TRUCK SAFETY

Is a fire truck near you? Listen to an adult. Stay safe so nobody gets hurt.

When a fire truck is going to an emergency, its lights and sirens are on. Drivers on the road must let the fire truck pass.

You should not bother firefighters when they are working. Do not get between them and their truck.

FIRE TRUCKS IN ACTION

Fire trucks are **vehicles** on the job.

They help save lives every day!

TOWER 49 LADDER
CHARDON FIRE DEPARTMENT
CHARDON

GLOSSARY

axes (AK-sez): tools with sharp blades on the end that firefighters use for making holes to enter buildings

connect (kuh-NEKT): to join together

emergencies (i-MUR-juhn-sees): sudden and dangerous situations that require quick action

fire extinguishers (fire ik-STING-gwish-urz): metal containers full of chemicals needed to put out fires

flashing (FLASH-ing): blinking on and off quickly

hydrant (HYE-druhnt): a large pipe in the street that supplies water to use for fighting fires

rescue (RES-kyoo): to save from danger

sirens (SYE-ruhnz): devices that make loud sounds to let people know that a fire truck is coming

telescopes (TEL-uh-skopes): moves up and down to become longer and shorter

22

vehicles (VEE-i-kuhlz): machines used to move people or things from one place to another

THINKING QUESTIONS

1. What is the job of a fire truck?

2. What equipment is found on a fire truck?

3. Why does a fire truck use both lights and a siren?

4. How can you stay safe around a fire truck?

5. Why are fire trucks important?

INDEX

ABOUT THE AUTHOR

Ryan James lives in the mountains of North Carolina where he goes hiking with his dog Bailey. He loves fly fishing, visiting farms in the area, and picking fresh produce. He has always enjoyed writing and wrote his first book as a teenager.